THE TROUBLE WITH NEW ENGLAND GIRLS

THE TROUBLE WITH NEW ENGLAND GIRLS

AMY MILLER

For John —
Great reading with
you again!
Amy Miller

Concrete Wolf
Louis Award Series

Concrete Wolf Louis Award Series

Poetry
ISBN 978-0-9964754-6-4

Design: Tonya Namura using Century Gothic (display) and
Minion Pro (text)

Cover art: *Edging Out at Sunset* by Laurie Justus Pace

Author photo by Megan Boone

Concrete Wolf
PO Box 445
Tillamook, OR 97141

http://ConcreteWolf.com

ConcreteWolfPress@gmail.com

For Frances Dampier, Peter Flynn,
Robert Burnham, Gwen Constant, Carol Abate,
Roberta Reynolds, and Truong Tran,
who taught what they loved.

Acknowledgments

Alehouse: "The Church of the Rowing Machine," "Sunnyvale"

Bellingham Review: "Why She Writes Sonnets"

Bird's Thumb: "To the Drone All Objects Are Beautiful"

Camas: "Monte Sereno," "The Sign at City View Road and City View Boulevard"

Cascadia Review: "Car Carrier"

Cider Press Review: "For Blossom, a $10 Hamster"

Cleaver: "Resistors"

Crab Orchard Review: "The Trouble with New England Girls"

Cultural Weekly: "'You Are Love and Light'"

Ghost Fishing: An Eco-Justice Anthology: "The Bee People"

Hippocrates Prize Anthology: "On Being Told My Brain Is the Normal Size"

The Hopper: "These Horses Will Not Be Harnessed"

Interrobang?!: "The Church of Desktop Computers"

Many Mountains Moving: "Fold"

Nimrod: "A Dream That Must Have Been My Father's," "this body"

Northwest Review: "A Parking Lot"

The Oregonian: "Sleeping Alone"

Raleigh Review: "Wolf OR-7 Fathers Three Pups," "Wolf OR-7 Passes the Site Where a Bounty Hunter Killed Oregon's Last Known Wolf in 1946," "Wolf OR-7 Shares a Carcass with Coyotes"

Rattle: "Channellock Pliers," "For Those Who Would Kill Chickens," "A Lullaby," "Rhode Island"

Sand Hill Review: "Prayer to the God of Landlords"

Spillway: "The Poet Laureate in the Laundromat," "Six Objects That Are Mine and One That Isn't"

Tinderbox Poetry Journal: "The Grief as the Universal Translator on *Star Trek*," "Mad Money," "Please Fill Out Form"

Willow Springs: "Lady's-Slipper"

ZYZZYVA: "Bike Path," "Bow Season," "Westfield, Massachusetts"

Some poems in this book first appeared in the chapbook *I Am on a River and Cannot Answer* (BOAT Press).

"I Am on a River and Cannot Answer" is based on an out-of-office message by Kimberley Barry.

The untitled river poems were originally written on postcards for the August Poetry Postcard Fest, founded by Paul Nelson and Lana Hechtman Ayers.

"The Grief as a Pattern of Black Dots on Purple Fabric" is for Karren Warren.

Thanks to Bev Miller and Steve Gable for the drone footage, and to all my writing workshopmates.

Table of Contents

THE TROUBLE WITH
NEW ENGLAND GIRLS

Westfield, Massachusetts

What would I do here?
Paint ladies' nails
in a gas-hot shop
out back of the mill.

Marry the man
who owns the Tool & Die,
loan my stepsons money,
write letters in the kitchen

long past the TV's last breath.
Even the snow
is gone to the sunken
bottommarsh of Crane Pond,

to the migrant watertips
of icicles off Granville Gorge.
This bristle-backed town,
this slasher-movie paradise

calls me
to the ice's edge,
covers me in sleet, tells me
what it could do:

set me down in a sleepy house
with the front porch falling in,
the dog dreaming on the rug.
It says I'll have to find

my own damned way
to make a living, my own
damned way home
if I have one.

A Parking Lot

I stayed kissed.
I said *god*, god
of the glacier letting go,
god that made the mouths
of Connecticut Valley men
strong after all that
rough weather. Hands
in your pockets, I pulled
you in. The air snapped
its ten-degree
fingers. Couldn't tell
if every crackmoney tramp
in town was yours
already, but then—black sky,
blue stars, naked heat
at the fingertip hollow
of your neck—
that was home,
that was here.
I live there now.
I stayed.

Prayer to the God of Landlords

Bless his half-empty head,
his hand that held
the Phillips screwdriver
he lost behind the hedge.

Bless the way he topped the trees,
the way he wanted them to be
perfect Grant Wood blow-pops.
Each day they show him sorrow:
peeling, sawed-off trunks,
severed necks above.

And bless the sound of his footsteps
on the ceiling at three a.m.,
the distant hiss of water, sounds
of him home from a trip
I'm sure went badly—traffic
and insolent weather,
forgotten skis and a flat
on Donner Pass—
but bless him anyway, home,
his gentle thumps of night,
the trail of creaks
leading off to his safe,
unmade bed.

My Ex Sends Me Photos of His Food

On a blue plate that was the one thing
his wife left him. Of meat and long-
simmered sauce. Of portions meted out
to last the week. Of spices hand-ground,
hand-warmed before he tosses them
in the scalding sea. Of the patient heads
of Brussels sprouts. Of his kitchen.

His mother says *You were so sad.*
His brother says *Why do you dredge that up?*
His father speaks from a small star
at the corner of the universe: *It was like
a death in the family.*

The one cake I baked him
was like a head crushed in a wreck.

Now we're all whiskey, whiskey,
whiskey on the phone. Forgive us
our trips into kitsch. Heineken
was so sixteen. We liked the girl
on St. Pauli, ready and busty and blue.

He sends me photos of a bush.
It's spring, and the bush is the shape
of a spaceship, glowing yellowish green like life
peeled off its skin and hurts in the open.
Maybe snow tomorrow. The world
is going backward, time in reverse. We're older
but the green beats of wings
still work, still hum. Soon
we'll taste apples, then berries.

To the Drone All Objects Are Beautiful

Especially the cattle, their shadows
black words against
the sage-green scrub. And the house
that could have been an armory,
parapets and ramparts that now,
closer, you see are wooly
trees. You can hear
the helicopter's flappy heart
beating ecstatic the egg of atmosphere,
see land and mountains bent
in the lens's milky pool. Two hills
that could hide a squadron
make a soft saddle
under sky. A long trench
dug by the square tooth
of a bulldozer is filled,
poor windowbox, with weeds.
Beside it a small dog runs,
raising a river of dust
toward a man standing
with something bulky in his hands
that turns out, on closer pass,
to be trowels and packets
of seeds.

Bow Season

The sky's burnt blue and the car jerks like a popcorn pop-per, on boulder on blitzen on woods rut crag hole. Some-body said there's a mansion out here but watch for hunters in their orange best, the deer in their silent stands, turkeys all American and sudden explosions of grouse. The road itself improbable, bend and lurch and skitter, bare trees reaching in December snap—gloves don't know the name of this cold. We're driving, a map in somebody's head, *it was here, I know it was up here somewhere over this rise* and out to this field and open and suddenly the view— Berkshire Berkshire Berkshire and that aching arching blue, not a wire not a smoke not even those everywhere mending walls. And then. The house. But ruins. Boulders dragged from a chimney, windows knocked out of a wall, tall escarpment of a second story, impudent trees in the kitchen, ground glass ground. Or was that the solarium, north light and a paintbrush touched to the tongue, or was that where the harp. Surely a harp. We wander and dust the filings of ancient weeds off corners of rock, wind pulling stone sockets. Only steps to the woods, but we stay close. The hunters. The season. We talk in hush of wheth-er arrows whistle, whether anyone ever hears a thing like that coming.

this body

pulls a little
to the left, starts slowly
some mornings after late
nights sorting broken

from rust. It swerves
from calling
anyone useless unless
it's a good joke or just

the metal truth,
the gut (in all
its glorious
schematics) turning

fitfully, fretfully over.
That is to say, this body
knows its holy-
shit collisions,

faint scrapes
and sideswipes (lucky
near and total quarter-
panel crumples),

                    burns
the ember of a touch
forever in its small
efficient tank.

The Poet Laureate in the Laundromat
for Lawson Fusao Inada

He stands to watch the comforter
hug and unhug itself
as the dryer muscles on and hums
its white-noise lullaby.
Even in the warm, overlit room,
he wears a leather jacket, hands
pushed deep in the pockets. Music,
perhaps, is what he hears
in the tinning and rumble,
notes dopplered to a shriek. Or poems,
spinning and powered
by their own unseen magnets.
He is not writing this down.
It washes over, river
and color and metal. But sometimes
something catches—
there, you can see—
he tilts his head, surprised.

Car Carrier

Some died quickly, snapped,
crushed, slender column shoved
through some important organ. This one

has a hole through its ribs, blue tarp
and tape for bandage. That one, lemon
Caddie, hasn't a scratch, some dad's

lark that didn't wake up
one morning. When the truck
turns at Tolman, you see the clean

red cube of the SmartCar has
another side, missing an eye and half
its face, one wheel crumpled

under the driver's seat,
the other three winched and stilled
by the muscular arms of chains.

Six Objects That Are Mine and One That Isn't

After a day of doctors and work
and money and even
the painstaking steering
to not hit that jerk
in the parking garage,
the soft hermetic
closing of my door sounds
like an army of angels
laying down their guns.
And my kitchen, the last
brown shards of sunset
sliding their blades
across the cabinets,
suddenly is paradise, the faucet
playing small creek music
as six objects on the sill—
two horses, a soapstone god,
the clock, the cup and bowl—
hold quiet court with the one
I'll never fully own, the plant
turning its panels to light
and mining a life
from its fistful of soil.

Rhode Island
for my mother

That summer in Misquamicut, when boys
as ripe as roadside corn shot pool in darkened
18-over bars, I found the joy
they buried deep in denim straight-front pockets—

pipe screens, joints, and all the damp and salty
wounded want my navigating hands
could plunder. Home and sunburned, bedroom walls
my gulag—no diary, no dolls—digging sand

and ashes from the trenches of my shoes,
I heard her laughing—late, in bed with Dad,
no malice in her voice, in love—a girl whose
moody boy came home for her with mad

martinis, seven jokes to sleep on, sleep
itself a garland he laid at her feet.

Lady's-Slipper

After we fought
you brought me an orchid
        small balloon
like a frog's throat
        frozen

we were in
        a deep
        green
        wood
        wires
of nettles and brambles

it's illegal to pick them,
you said,
        the flower floating
        severed
        surprised
on a brown stem

as if
        you would
        kill
        you would bend
        the law
        into
        a locket

and leave it
in a red box
             inside
my screen door
             at dawn

you did that
             once

A Lullaby

Sleep now. The city
you were building in your head,
its shouting and conveyances,
its strikers and unhelpful signs,
its cops with their stern citations,
rest. Rest the piteous call
from your sister and the words
you boiled in the pot
all day.

       Somewhere
deer fatten in a sudden
thaw. A lake floats hundreds
of Russians in bathing suits.
And your dreams—no one can take
those wild paintings
and unbelievable music,
or your lashes dropping
their feathers, or the factory
of your own lungs,
quietly working into the night.

A Dream That Must Have Been My Father's

One saw was mine—
silver and sharp-toothed,
a hand-carved handle I lifted
to the peg. Up
in the rafters' dark,
I saw another—
Who leaves beauty behind?—
hanging from a hole
in its venerable blade.
I lifted it down,
and I swear
it purred like a fed cat,
my whole shop humming.
Nails in their boxes
waited to rain like arrows
on an unsure enemy.
The rope I'd coiled
around one arm
lay like a sleepy centerfold.
The room itself was metaphor,
the firebox of my dreaming.
No one came
to speak to me there,
no one sat tall
on the high stool,
watching the sawdust land
like snow
on the cold floor.

In the distance you hear it:
an engine of consequence. Fuels
igniting. A race? A rocket?
A war? A roar like great bodies
boiled. Then round the swifting turn
of the river, and there—white churn,
frenzied water hills, a permanent
rain rising—and you're in it,
down the pitching stairs. You knew
this would come. You knew it.

The Grief as the Universal Translator on *Star Trek*

Say *father* and it says
first horse.
Say *my love*
and it says *the wild.*
These planets are all
my planets, their tongues
my lost and speeding insect songs.
Come on, Scotty,
everybody dies in the stirred-up gel
of somebody's transporter.
Haven't you ever beamed back
divided? And what's this backward
language now? It says
my baby's gone missing
when all that blew up
was a world.

If you fall into the rapids,
make an arrow with your feet.
Make a pillow of everything
behind you. Look up. Hang on
to that one buoyant stick
you brought. Remember,
you may not hear voices
above the water. If you know
you're drowning—*Is this air,
or again that dream?*—
before it's too late, make an X
with your arms—think crossbones—
which almost anyone can do,
even if one is broken.

The Grief as a Small Wooden Box

You carry it with one hand under,
one over. In the rain, you pull
a flap of your coat to hide it,
though you're not sure
what's in there. Sounds
like gravel. Today
it's embarrassing, so old world,
drab and flat while all above you
spring tongues open her green.
You see others with their boxes,
their pinpoint concentration,
minding their steps on the curbs,
the cracks that could break them.
To drop it—how unthinkable.
How delicious.

Someone is scarred. Someone sliced
three purple lips across a leg—a rock,
a paddle, a fight's metal edge. No sun
could ever smooth them, dangling
from a boat, loose in the pitch
and bend. Pain? No matter. Smile back
at the river. The eagle
is missing some feathers. The clouds
are never this shape again.

The Grief as a Caribbean Cruise while Reading a Romance Novel

That is to say, go fuck yourselves,
petty worries and the slipping shale
of the past's impossible shoulders.
I don't care who's watching me read
or who wants to sell me happiness
in two tight t-shirts and a seashell-
bustiered mermaid. The sea
climbs over itself, and the many-
eyed creatures in its gut
are all business. A vast
indifference waits, salt face, line
dividing life from space. The meals
are never really free. You're paying.
You just don't know it.

This town is full of Harleys
and harlots, skinny kids
and a brown retriever
on a rope. The barking. They fish
the mercurial river, swim
in the washed-up soup
of the old mine. Cold stares
as they wade at the boat ramp,
watching the tour group back
a raft on a trailer
into the water. They stand
in that exhaust,
breathing it deep.

The Grief as the Warning Siren for Hosler Dam

This is a test. In the event of your own
emergency, you will be instructed
how to scream, where to dump
your ill-constructed sandbags.
You may not know which side
of the river to climb, or whether
fitness is a virtue. Be prepared
to wade into water and then, too late,
change your mind. Pack
comforting items—some books,
a blanket. But be aware
that patience kills. And so does
panic. Somewhere in between
you'll see a boat, inviting
in its listlessness. For God's sake,
do not board it. In the event
the debris wash carries you
out to sea, please look around
for your belongings. We all belong
to someone. Someone
may be missing you. This
may also be a test.

Fire stole the summer and smoke
laid its tail in the valley for weeks.
But after rain—washed blue, bright cloud,
and air so full of trees it even breathes
the past. We found again the basement—
half-remembered arguments and photos
brittle with fear. We held our faded faces
to each other in the light.

The Grief as a One-Way Mirror

Today I'm the cop
just watching
that tweet tweet tweet alone
in the room.
I'm out here all day.
I come
from a long line
of detectives.
There—
did you see it flinch?
That little bird in there
is flesh. Tomorrow
we'll trade places.
I'll be the echo
thrown against the glass.
Not now. This
is about a few hours
of control.

I am on a river and cannot answer.
I crawled here in a pickup
under Douglas fir and spruce
that steepled their hands over
delicate cores. I cannot hear
your message now. Please leave
a sliver of yourself in the soft fur
of bark along the banks
where I will be living.

The Grief as a Pattern of Black Dots
on Purple Fabric

You wore this dress.
You made it
gorgeous, dots puckered
at the waist and meeting
the broken-bone line
where the surgeon
winched you open,
small swords drawing everywhere
the floodlines of your body.
I see you
in between the black—
remember purple's taste?
A sweeter than grape,
plum tart—yes,
a thinning skin's embrace
that covers like a cloth.
The pattern moves.
Dots gather, a mass,
then vanish.

Was it mink or otter,
wet and watching our boat
slide by? Loosestrife, bright
on purple ropes, strangling
the willows' roots, long toes
in the river. Someone said
a huge salmon and the current—
brown of fire and silt—
swallowed and spit
and fish—three fish!—
showed fins in sun
as I pulled my hand
through the water's pelt.

The Grief as a Low Depression over Southern Indiana

A year's worth of rain
already. Vines climb
whatever doesn't move. Heavy
was only a word before the roof
stove in. Hunters are too hot
and the limestone quarry stands
quiet as history. Clouds fight fast
and boil a wall. Flash
and roll and it's like
somebody pulled a rope and let
an ocean fall down. Pull over.
It may never stop but you can't
drive in all this mess, so loud
it drowns the radio's
wail. You're inside, alone,
your own lone breath making weather
on the windows. Lights on
so nobody hits you
as they carom this way
under their own insistent storms.

Because the powerhouse stares dead
with a face full of old bricks, and the river
spikes with a spiny rust of Rebar,
and turbines never made a sound
worth hearing, we ask that the salmon
rename the rapids they run through now
with their pulsing flanks and single
compass point. Maybe they'll say it,
now that the wall is gone, when they leap
in front of the boat, their skins
reflecting watery suns as they climb
back up the mountain.

The Grief as the Theory of Parallel Universes

You have taken this drive before.
But the roadmarks aren't
what you remember: That station
where you had to stop
is now an office. The doctor
is now a cop. The papers
were yellow before and now
(miraculous electric angels)
the nurses know you by name. You
are the constant, but even
your memory remakes itself.
Remember, you were stopped there,
the engine out of breath.
Today you're still moving.

Come see this mountain. Where once
white nothings of smoke descended—
stoned milk, blown chalk—now, the sharpened
teeth of trees. And cattle and a road—no,
a waterway long dry. What clear country
docks against us? Unfamiliar clean,
blue-blue assaulting increments
of the eye, a gold grass August.
There, distance. A hawk,
small but unmistakably rising.

Channellock Pliers

They came in a box
Dad gave me one Christmas,
nestled among the level
and awl and putty knife
and changeable screwdriver
and wire cutters and tin snips.
I went home and weighed
each in my hand and finally
put the channellocks
under my pillow,
their heft just right
for splitting a skull
in a blind swing
out of a startled sleep.
I never told my father
this. Their handles
dipped in red rubber still hush
their clank when I hold them
in the night.

Please Fill Out Form

Date of birth
An astronaut hanging from heaven.
Doctors gone, empty halls
in a new hospital.

Chief complaint
The body's box
shut—
a second, silent mind.

Known allergies
This rough patch. Who knows
what landed first? Or crept
from the inside out.

Family history
Eight pins.
There—half down.
Four pins.
Atrocious game, dark
rolling in from the distance.

Reproductive history
He never would have stayed.

On Being Told My Brain Is the Normal Size

Of course you think of Einstein,
his brain in a jar under that doctor's sink
all those years, acorn pried
from the dry shell of his body
and rinsed in the church of science.
His was giant, a universe
with recordably more matter
that someone saved,
then forgot. And you can't help thinking

of putting it in someone else's old body,
Einstein in somebody's
big head, the careful reattachments,
the brain's surprise
to find itself back on the beach,
peering at the soft bright, sharp bright
spines of creatures fixed in tidepools,
their fluids just awash enough
to bathe them in lunch and dinner.

Later, the brain will see the miracle
of Walgreen's at 10 p.m., the bright gum packs
and bored cashier and Coke cans and bologna
preserved at just below
the decomposing temperature.
The brain will like the cold outside,
the turn of the key in the quiet ignition,
the street that leads home
through houses half asleep.

I only thought of this today,
two weeks after I waited
inside the magnet's telescope,
XTC in the headphones,
the stars and planets of my head

held still for the clattering cameras.
And now, having seen the charts—
it was only a galaxy, no
dark matter at all—in this new time
when turning on the TV is a wonder,
when steam on the kitchen window
is an indisputable sign of life,

I think of Einstein
and that sad cashier at Walgreen's
in her green uniform
and hope that whatever she has or thinks she has
will soon be gone and she'll walk
out of that store at the end of her shift
to find the sun's come up,
and even though it's cold
and her car is brittle with ice,
it starts,
it starts.

Sunnyvale

He came home to two martinis
and Art Buchwald out loud
in his black bucket chair,
steam creeping out the kitchen door.
By dinner he'd rolled his sleeves,
brown arms like snakes under skin,
and we knew to pass the plates
without a sound.
If he was happy, he'd tell us
about the railroad—
emptied the toilets
right onto the tracks—
or the slaughterhouse
or the aircraft carrier nose-up
and falling fast.
Fish sticks hung in mid-air
and crashed the conning towers
of our tater tots. Milk bled out
the mouths of glasses.
Later, he'd change
and walk to the garage,
wrestle metal for hours
and shoot the bright rivets
through round, clean holes.

Helium

Somewhere outside Amarillo
is a tank my brother will use.
He's told me how it works:
the bag, the collar made of tape.
Five seconds, and you're out.
No *brains like scrambled eggs.*

The gas fields breathe and everything's
collected. Farther down, it's rock
and smaller pockets, less
and less in history's
narrowing light.

My brother climbs a ladder,
flushes gutters, paints the eaves,
hips protesting in their sockets.
It's not so much the dying
but the *weak and bloody wait.*

Somewhere outside Amarillo
the particles excite at lifting
and expanding, the lost balloons
they'll tangle in the lines. Small voices,
smaller, comical, sealed under plastic's
pinch. Great plains of opening
and thunder.

It's not so much can't hack it
as *can't remember shit.* Not
that my brother's forgetting—
our father's pee-filled shoes,
the drive out there every Sunday.
It's not so much for now

or next month. My brother's
just arranging. He got
the box in the mail, the bag
and typed directions. The tank
is out there somewhere, outside
Amarillo. It's on his list to get.

"You Are Love and Light"
handwritten sign on a laundromat wall

You are also that crazy jitterbrained fuck
they called the cops on, loud and scared
and pulling your love on its tangled cord
right up out of your throat and hurling it straight
at that small woman when you hissed
You stole my sweatshirt, the good one.

The sign on the other wall,
Be kind and forgiving,
this was for me. It was not
for the tall man
who did his Jesus best
to talk you off the roof
your brain was walking. Also not
for the cop whose radio
pinned to his shoulder said
these visions were old
and he had only to quell them
down to quiet talk that would not
make the news tonight.

It was for me, *forgiving*, as I stood against
the washer and tried not to think how drunks
come out at four, something about Oprah
or the end of *Magnum, P. I.* or some other
comforting greenbacked bull choking
every satellite dish in the trailer park. It is not
for the mother with three kids or the college
couple mingling their underwear.

No, *kind*, this was for me
as I skirted the raggled
mess of you, even your eyes
at odds, blinking and unblinking
and not quite taking in
the cop, his shuttered gun,
the manager (who knows
the cant and whine of every
unbalanced machine) and me,
sidling my basket out the door
and trying not to fuel
the spell of all of our wild
intimate unraveling.

The Sign at City View Road
and City View Boulevard

Here is the road I dreamed full of tractors.
The carrots that fell off the truck, just there,

that we picked up later, their pocked skins slick
and red with rain. Here is the rain, cauldrons of cloud,

our arms tingling with lightning as we waited
on the lawn for a storm to the west

to dump its belly. There
is the stable, now full of potatoes,

stone from the cold rebellion.
And as for the sign, our neighbor screwed

with anyone not from this town
and turned it ninety degrees

so they'd come back in their cars,
puzzled, pointing, flapping their maps

while he watched from his front window,
a Stanley steel mug of coffee

on the breakfast table
he made from an old barn door.

Resistors

He taught me how to bend their arms
so they stayed. To solder them
solid with lead and resin, perfect
alchemical drops. Each striped
in mathematical candy—purple
for seven, green for five—it took
a simple decoder. But how
to speak to me, his daughter
striped in a thrift-store skirt
and punk shoes, this was more
like the keening barrel rolls
of his cropdusting days.
He showed me the logs,
brown old books with his pencil
scratch: *take-off, touch-and-go,*
spins, loops, spins. Then back
to the workbench to assemble
more boards, the great dumb
heads of capacitors looming
over the small resistors,
all of them holding on.

Wolf OR-7 Passes the Site
Where a Bounty Hunter Killed
Oregon's Last Known Wolf in 1946

The air was moved, and air
has memory. The things
it hears: a bullet
shattering, bone's bark
riven. Echo and wave,
a round bowl rung forever.
And scent—triggers
and flash, 280 million
receptors set mysteriously
waving. Buried
in the bog of an old
pine slough that feeds
the Umpqua, there—
fine scrapings, iron stain
a trunk still tries
to hide. A fleck.
An atom. A gash.

Bike Path

half of us are sure
who did it
       sun-stained face
       half feral   where
       would he hide
       a blade that big
       winter   in his coat

when the doorbell
           rings
I have to think
       where
is that wreath
does it block
the hole
I would see him through
       voice
says clear
says loud
       it's me
       it's Mary
       your neighbor

in the grocery store
a man
so kind
       the cashier
       blushes as she takes
       his money
his face
       flushed
from walking
or wind
       a killer
       eats too
       what would he buy?

outside, in the dark
        our bags   our meat
        our apples and razors
we could hide
and do anything
even
watch each other   close
from behind
        windshield glass

somebody hacked
        the trees up good
for days
        they walked the path
in rubber gloves
        pressing plaster
        in cut marks

paper tiger
        in the neighbor's
        window   wasn't
        there
before   beautiful
        way to not
                see
        not see
               in

walking home
        he must
have heard
              something
behind him

I loved
        that trail
how it winds
        past the little
campfire
spot   out
        into oaks
        and madrones
I might have
        met a dog
        a man
        said hello
        kept walking

Why She Writes Sonnets

Because she likes the way the daisies slip
their flowering hands between the stern fence boards.
Because her grandmother told her of bloodied lips
and roped hands when the soldiers dragged her toward
their tents while her sisters huddled in the kitchen
wearing their ugliest clothes. Because her feet
like shoes, and if it weren't for the walls of their pension,
she and her husband would stagger into the street.
Because the needlework stretched tight on the hoop
bleeds bright colors. Even her voice,
born in its box, sometimes takes the leap
up to soprano, crow-caw, Jericho brass.
Because she lies at night at the center of four
posts, a kind man heavy beside her.

Wolf OR-7 Shares a Carcass with Coyotes

Uneasy. Torn. Contentious
brothers not brothers.
Who are we but stars
of our own wilderness?
There was baring and approach,
thrust, feign, a show
of who had the upper hand.
Then reversal. I forget
who won. That taste—
something so long dead
and needles of hunger so hot
that I have to say
it was paradise, that mouthful
ripped in the presence
of who cares who,
their eyes hard on me
and waiting their turn.

Mad Money

She says it's for bus fare home. Not like crazy,
paint the town, but mad mad really mad,
hornets and hell and how could he

And the fog was so thick they had to stop
and sleep in the car. In the morning they
saw they'd been hanging over the edge of a

Says you tuck it in a shoe in case he takes
your purse, in case a hand goes over
your mouth as one goes up your

Says her aunt brought home these sailors
and they all played poker and her aunt
died a drunk but she always liked a

And the car got a flat and he was in a cast
and he changed it with a broken

And somebody stole his shirt and his watch
but they went to Reno and got married
in a borrowed

She says even then you tuck it in a drawer
in case he

Monte Sereno

When I had two spoons,
the kitchen was a bathroom,
the closet was a cupboard.
The fridge tuned its fork,
lonesome in the shed. In rain,
the roses splayed and bricks
forgot their mortar. I had

one knife, a saw,
and somebody's old hammer. Rats
made feast of the rafters,
frost brought the moon
and the brown moving
backs of coyotes. I had
two bowls and a steel
teapot ticking,
ticking on the warm
burner in the dark.

The Trouble with New England Girls

They think the moon rises
and sets. They speak English
as if English were their one
true tongue.
       They have hair
and they have teeth
and sometimes they wear
bad sweaters
          missing a button.
They live in houses
with mothers for the most part,
brothers, dads,
         dogs
patrolling the yards.
Sometimes they drive out
under the moon.
Sometimes they get pregnant
and drive to New Jersey
and sometimes
       they come back
married and quiet,
or quiet and alone.
Sometimes they steal
the bus fare
      to get there
and back.
      They feel the ocean
pinning the wrists of the land,
the stars
looking down, unblinking,
          the moon
with its third-degree light
pounding the truth
right out of them.

They wish
they were Baja girls
shimmering on a beach,
not a bus or sweater
in sight,
and the moon
        far up there
where it belongs.

These Horses Will Not Be Harnessed

They just brought lightning down
on the ignorant heads of teasel and thorn. They flew
out of a country you helped to make, then beat
the brainpan's old assumptions dead. The whip is history
they remember, the fence, the kick, the rope.
They dreamed the end of anger together—such ripples
and touch, such brush and elegant angle of pastern,
of ear. They are beautiful. They know this.
They speak in an ever-longer pattern
that they themselves invented, born of torque
and tongue.
                Yes, you may be threatened. Yes,
you may wake up suddenly surrounded by horses.
Some may leap over you. Some
may breathe on you hard. Some may turn
and show you the whirling universe of an eye.
I can't tell you what will happen next.
I can't tell you what to do.

Fold

I love those big yellow tables
in laundromats, big enough
for slow, soft sex among
the folded towels and t-shirts,
smooth and swept
as heaven's floor
from all those years of clean,
from the up-close scrutiny
of everyone's imperfections: frayed jeans,
torn socks in the flat,
fluorescent light.

                Each of us lost
in our contemplative folding, if we think
of our warm union—
that living here, breathing here,
eyes closed, our clothes
the mountain kingdom of our sleep—
if we are thinking this, our thoughts
are tumbling on themselves
in our own sealed bodies,
each door a window and a lock
with a whirling life inside.

Sleeping Alone

Listening
to the neighbor's dog
bark
and bark.
He must
be very big,
his mouth as big
as my head,
his head
as big
as a Macy's Day float,
his corridor throat
commanding me
to hear:
I am one
dog
in the lonely bowl
of night
and there
is so
much
dark.

Horses Run

not just
evolution's darling   not only
the smart one who opens
        the stall door with a long
        persistent nimble   no
that slow one too

ran right out from under
my sorry

        flipped at the slightest
        his bullet of a body
        dragging me the flea
        on his arcing bucking

then head-
ass over backward   I was dust
and a bucket
of bruise, one finger sideways
got up
        to count
        the broken   they run

in the mind's
old movie
        punched
        in the card
of every blinking,
blindered, elegant
hayswept brain

        older

than any rope

For Those Who Would Kill Chickens

I wish I could show you
how we saved him. Named him
Steven, stupid name
for a chicken, but
when he wandered
out from the woods,
black sheen hooked
with leaves and the crazy
red rubber of his comb,
we had to call him
something. I thought
Lucky after a horse
stomped him so hard—
caught in the corral
like a mouse in traffic—
then maybe Rip
when he tucked his head
in the elbow of the foreman's
wife and fell asleep
in her arms. *Steven*,
she whispered—who knows,
some baby or a friend
long gone—and it stuck.
I could show you
my sandwiches he pulverized,
his crooked Jagger dance
on the paddock's dusty stage,
how each of us came
to grudgingly help
this alien flown from some
coop, how a thing
like that takes root
on a shelf in a dark
tack room, settling

on an overshirt you meant
to take home that now
is sacrificed—no matter—
to this thing you've named,
that needs you. Each night
we closed and locked
that door against whatever
was out there
that hadn't yet learned
his name or the iridescence
of his weak and perfect wings.

The Bee People

They sat quiet while the council droned
about the ugly new plaza
and knots of traffic
tying up North Main.
They sat in their sandals
and blue t-shirts painted
with the tiger backs of bees
and waited for the vote
about hives and lots and setbacks
and neighbor notification
and EpiPens and the relative
aggression of wasps and the range
of the average working bee
and colony collapse and fields
east of the rain shadow. Some
hummed. One trembled. I noticed
their hair, a golden sheen
on every head as if the bees
had somehow had a hand
in getting them here, had pushed them
down the walk with wings
that hovered, translucent and precise,
and steered them by the sun
to where they had to go.

The Church of Desktop Computers

He says
they're all born
with a kind of cancer,
ones and zeroes dropped
from the garlands of their code,
each replication minutely
misremembered.

Dialing
small screws
with a jeweler's held breath,
he pries off the plate
and beholds the slots,
imperfect mouths
made ready.

The gray box,
he knows, is the flesh
but not the soul, a house
radiant with worries,
dimming even now,
its voice a disconsolate choir
that doesn't like
new songs. He patches,
replaces, blows dust
from its fan.

In the end,
even he will be forgotten,
his small tool box
packed and loaded in the car,
driving home to his wife
who sometimes wonders
who he is when she sees
his graceful hands

setting dishes on the shelf,
pouring tea from the kettle
that he just now stopped
from screaming.

Wolf OR-7 Fathers Three Pups

Used to be such a sheep killer.
Used to howl all hours and stalk
the gullies. Drank
some crazy moonlight alone. Now
this tether, small cries,
damp tang, defensible den. To say
they wear off your sharp edges
presumes they have powers
more than tumble and yip.
And maybe they do, their ears
already knowing my chuff,
imprinted with a joy that only
the end of hunger makes.
To think I once called
and a hundred miles of no one
would answer.

For Blossom, a $10 Hamster

Your God will know you
by the slant of your one white spot
and the way you don't cry out
when lifted from your cardboard cage
by the giant hand of a five-year-old girl.

In your two months you already
have become secretly pregnant,
the dials of your soft body
spinning through their complications
in the slave cells of the pet store.

Think, if you were rare, the distant sightings
and cataloguing, your steep and cordoned
habitat, the teams debating your very
existence on that clean pin-top of land.
Instead you, born in a clutch of sisters,

known only by your crooked spot
(though to your sisters you smelled like you
and your name was never Blossom),
here you are sleeping on sawdust
the girl tries so hard to keep clean,

and though she is not your God,
she lays a finger on you late at night
to feel your warm pulsar of breath.
And when the mean boy comes over to play,
she hides your box under the bed

and says you ran away,
her face on fire with the lying
she does for you, Blossom, as if

you were the last of your kind
on Earth, and she
was the only one who knew.

The Church of the Rowing Machine

In the end,
I arrive backward—
not the way I learned it
in the book,
but pulled by the body's
wordless logic,
lever and bone.
I can see where I began,
the shore of a dream lake
where I put in every morning.
My crewmates sweat
and huff and secretly fear
I won't keep up, but they
are illusion
and distance is illusion,
the water, the carpet
rolling to meet my strokes.
Books kneel on shelves,
chairs have parted with their ghosts.
The door is open
to the rest of the house,
the otherworld of day.
Behind me—who knows
what's coming? Who can say
I haven't moved an inch?
I tell you, I saw the reeds
slide by. I heard
the ducks on wings
nearly graze my shoulder
as they rowed
the invisible air.

About the Author

Amy Miller grew up in northern California and western Massachusetts. She worked as a ranch hand, photographer's assistant, health-food-store bookkeeper, and electronic assembler before finding a home in publishing with *Guitar Player* magazine, where she worked for 14 years. Since then she has had a long career as an editor and print-production manager at several magazines, book publishers, and the Oregon Shakespeare Festival.

Her poetry and nonfiction have appeared in *Gulf Coast*, *Nimrod*, *Permafrost*, *Rattle*, *Tinderbox*, *Willow Springs*, and *ZYZZYVA*, as well as *Asimov's Science Fiction*, *Fine Gardening*, *The Poet's Market*, and many anthologies, including *Nasty Women Poets* and *Clash by Night: A* London Calling *Anthology*. Her chapbooks include *I Am on a River and Cannot Answer* (BOAAT Press) and *Rough House* (White Knuckle Press). She won the Cultural Center of Cape Cod National Poetry Competition, judged by Tony Hoagland, the Jack Grapes Poetry Prize from *Cultural Weekly*, The *Whiskey Island* Prize, the Kay Snow Award, and the Earl Weaver Baseball Writing Award.

She lives in Ashland, Oregon.